SWEET, SHARP,
AND STRONG

SWEET, SHARP, AND STRONG

A Review of N. T. Wright's
Surprised by Scripture

DOUGLAS WILSON

BLOG & MABLOG
PRESS AND TIRE CENTER
MOSCOW, IDAHO

Blog & Mablog Press and Tire Center
Moscow, Idaho
www.dougwils.com

Cover design and interior layout: Valerie Anne Bost
Cover images: Unsplash.com/Patrick Tomasso (books), FreeImages.com/ Caroline Hoos (texture)

Version: 20230916Print

For Uncle Everett

THE MABLOG
BOOK REVIEW SERIES

O n his website, *Blog and Mablog* (dougwils.com), the author has from time to time written extensive, chapter-by-chapter reviews of books that, to his way of thinking, needed such a thorough interaction. As these in-depth critiques are collected into this series of books, the blogginess of them will remain. References to prior posts and comments will pop up, the *nows* are really *thens*, and so forth. Numbers in parentheses refer throughout to pages in the book under scrutiny.

ABOUT THE TITLE

Since we first began publishing the Mablog Book Review Series, Amazon has changed its policy regarding titles of books that contain the titles of other books. So we have obligingly changed the titles in the series, relegating the other fellows' titles to small print in our subtitles. If you bought this because you were under the impression it was a new book, we are very sorry about that. But it was cheap. Try to keep some perspective.

For this volume, the new title comes from Ezekiel 3:1, where the prophet eats the Word and finds it sweet as honey, and Hebrews 4:12, where Paul likens the Word to a sharp and powerful sword.

CONTENTS

GAUTAMA
AND THE ANT WAR

I t has been a while, I might note, since I have worked through a book chapter by chapter. Even though no one has been clamoring for it, they ought to have been, and so here I am with another one. The book I have selected was just released by HarperOne, and is N.T. Wright's latest—*Surprised By Scripture*.[1] The format of the book—an assembly of edited lectures around various topical themes (the subtitle is "Engaging Contemporary Issues")—lends itself to my approach here. Each chapter stands alone, and so each installment of mine will similarly stand alone.

1 N.T. Wright, Surprised by Scripture: Engaging Contemporary Issues (San Francisco: HarperOne, 2014).

The first chapter is on the relationship of faith and science. In his treatment of this subject, Wright says some things that are quite insightful, and he says some other things that are hopelessly confused. And on that note, let me declare my intentions early on. What I want to do, working through this book, is give credit where credit is due (and there look to be chapters where I will largely be a cheerleader) and to cut no slack where slack oughtn't be cut (for there look to be chapters, like this one, where he gets the essential point upside down).

His basic argument in this chapter is that the modern world is in thrall to an updated form of Epicureanism, and that this causes us to misunderstand the nature of faith/science integration. He wants us to undergo a "radical rethink" of the whole debate, instead of focusing on what side of the debate (in the older forms of it) we think we are on.

Another related problem he addresses, albeit not so directly, is *What shall we do about the Americans?* "I want to point out that the way the science and religion debate is conducted and perceived in North America is significantly different from the ways analogous debates are conducted and perceived elsewhere" (2).

This is quite true, but there is perhaps another explanation than the one he provides. But before getting to that, here is his statement on that same matter that I think is quite insightful: "The cultural polarization in American society, including the fundamentalist-modernist controversy of the first half of the twentieth century, has roots that go back at least as far as the Civil War in the 1860s" (4).

I think this is right on the money, and it is closely related to the broader culture war issues, as Wright points out elsewhere in this chapter. There are many battles, but there is only one war. Wright and I look at the same phenomenon, and we both agree that it is occurring. But he feels sorry for us, and I don't.

> This is why I say that, though of course the issues have been important elsewhere in the world, Americans seem to have had a particularly hard time of it. (5)

> The present American context, which reflects these culture wars in newer forms, makes these issues much harder for Americans to deal with than they are for the rest of us. (6)

But there is another way to take all this. I certainly do agree that there is an ongoing fight over these things in America that we do not see elsewhere. But mightn't it be because American Christians have not surrendered and are still fighting? Of course the struggle is harder for a soldier who is still being a soldier. The fight is difficult for those who didn't quit the difficulty. That's not a bug. It's a feature. Wright says that these things are "much harder" for us. He says we have had a "particularly hard time of it." Okay. But Paul told Timothy to "endure hardship as a good soldier of Jesus Christ" (2 Tim. 2:3).

Of course, there is such a thing as unnecessary hardship. There is faithfulness hard, and there is stupid hard (Prov. 13:15). So the question then becomes whether we American Christians are having a hard time because of our hard heads, or whether we are having a hard time because the hardness in question is in our backbone. To determine *that* we need to move to consider the rest of Wright's discussion.

He then moves to a very helpful discussion of Epicureanism, and he shows how the whole modernity project is simply Epicureanism 2.0. This whole section is very good, but after he rode this bike around the block several times, he unfortunately started to wobble.

He quotes philosopher Catherine Wilson to the effect that in the modern world we are all Epicureans now. Wright then adds, "It is the default mode, sadly, for most Christians who oppose modern science as well as for scientists who oppose modern Christianity" (11).

Wait, what? This is absolutely the kind of thing you need an argument for. But not only does Wright make the assertion without an argument, he does so with the calm serenity of Gautama looking at an ant war. But if Epicureanism is "no gods or absent gods," then you cannot just say that those who espouse this are Epicureans, "not to mention those who hotly oppose it." By this handy device I could prove that Robert E. Lee fought for the North.

If I had to *guess* at what argument he might make, I would reconstruct it from a few bits and pieces he left for us here and there. For example, he says: "That is why, I think, some of those who insist on God's actions in creation and providence, who see him as a God who is essentially outside the whole process and who reaches in, despite the Epicurean prohibition, and does things for which there was otherwise no cause, sound quite shrill" (15–16).

While he does grant that those who deny Epicureanism are not Epicureans in the *technical* sense, he still argues that "in science/religion debates or evolution/creation debates, it is all too easy for the scientists or evolutionists to state their position in Epicurean terms, *and for the Christians or creationists to follow suit*" (14, emphasis his).

By this he appears to mean that if Christians believe in a "supernatural" realm, across which God reaches, even if He reaches across it every minute of every day, they have ceded way too much to their adversaries. Wright dismisses "supernaturalists who want to make him [Jesus] the divine 'invader' from 'beyond,' performing miracles to prove his supernatural power and summoning us to leave this world and return with him to his. These pictures simply reflect the false either/or of Epicureanism" (23).

He complicates things further because, near the bottom of page 14, he makes a frightful muddle of the definition of miracles and providence. In Scripture, God is the one in whom we live and move and have our being (Acts 17:28). Christ is the one in whom all things hold together (Col. 1:18). Not only did He create the world *ex nihilo*, but He also sustains it in existence every moment "by the word of his power" (Heb. 1:3). God is not absent or distant. But despite my high Calvinism with regard to numbered hairs and fallen sparrows and the stray leaf skittering down the street in the autumn breeze, its every turn foreordained before all worlds, I would say this robust view of God's ongoing providence must leave room for God acting in ways that have no antecedent secondary causes in the created order. Take the Incarnation, for example. That was God reaching in from outside. *Creatio ex nihilo* reaches from outside, by definition.

Now suppose Wright is simply wanting to deny the notion that most things run by impersonal natural law, but that when God reaches in and does something direct, "it's a miracle." If that is all he is saying, then he is correct. The only problem *then* would be that it would be an annoying instance of Wright's habit of acting like he has discovered distinctions that have been theological commonplaces for centuries. He is like an astronomer who has been working on his telescope (quite ably) for decades, but who keeps claiming to have discovered the moon. We could let that go, but he keeps trying to name it. But other people, turns out, have telescopes too, and some people have noticed the moon without any formal training at all. He is like the man in Boswell's *Life of Johnson*, concerning whom Johnson said that he sat down to write a book, in which he told the world a number of things which the world had been, all his life, trying to tell him.

The biblical stance is that God sustains *everything* we see in nature, and sometimes He performs "signs" that cannot be accounted for by means of antecedent causes in providence.

Having identified the enemy as Epicureanism, he wants to show some fight, but apparently without any actual fighting. If you start actually fighting, someone might mistake you for an American.

"Once we recognize the deep-rooted Epicureanism of much of modern Western culture, our vocation as Christian thinkers is not to make an easy, compromising peace with it but to discern how to restate and reinhabit a genuinely Christian worldview in its place" (18).

I would suggest that there is absolutely no way to do this while retaining the respect of the Epicurean establishment. And that means you have to be willing to be called a fundamentalist.

"And this means that everything we might say about the relationship between heaven and earth, between God and the world, between faith and science, between piety and public life—all those analogous questions that have so baffled Western modernism—find their answer in Jesus" (22). I am not about to argue with that, at least not with the Jesus part, but I do want to conclude by pointing out a problem with one of the phrases—"faith and science."

All those pairs but one are what they are. Heaven and earth, God and the world, piety and public life. And I agree with Wright that they can be brought together in a coherent whole only through Jesus. A thousand amens.

But "faith and science" is a pair not like the other pairs. Faith in what? Which science? Those are two bottles that can be filled with any number of fluids, and I want to know what those fluids are before I start trying to integrate anything. "Science" contains conclusions, doctrines. Scientists teach certain things, and they do in the name of science. So before I try to harmonize anything, I want to ascertain that what I am harmonizing my scriptural understanding with is actually true. I am prepared to harmonize my views of Scripture with the germ theory of disease. I am not prepared to harmonize my views of Jesus walking on water with a doctrine that says such things never happen. But both are advanced with the embossed seal of "The Science Is Settled" on them. Shoot, things are so crazy these days that this thing called "climate change" has even gotten that seal.

This is why reconciling "faith and science" is like taking on the task of reconciling "faith and stuff taught in books."

AND NOW FOR A LITTLE
FALSE TEACHING . . .

We now proceed down the hallway to the second chapter of *Surprised by Scripture*. The question posed here concerns whether we really need a historical Adam, and the answer, as far as I can make out, is no, probably not. At the end of his reasoning, Wright says, "I do not know whether this is exactly what Genesis meant or what Paul meant," but the line of reasoning he suggested "leads me in that direction" (38).

But if he is uncertain about what he is putting forward, the uncertainty vanishes when talking about young earth creationists who differ with him. Wright was surprised by Scripture. I was surprised to find me and my kind numbered among the Jehovah's Witnesses.

> I wonder whether we are right even to treat the young-earth position as a kind of allowable if regrettable alternative, something we know our cousins down the road get up to but which shouldn't stop us getting together at Thanksgiving . . . And if, as I suspect, many of us don't think of young-earthism as an allowable alternative, is this simply for the pragmatic reason that it makes it hard for us to be Christians because the wider world looks at those folks and thinks we must be like that too? Or is it—as I suggest it ought to be—because we have glimpsed a positive point that urgently needs to be made and that the young-earth literalism is simply screening out? That's the danger of false teaching: it isn't just that you're making a mess; you are using that mess to cover up something that ought to be brought urgently to light. (31)

Golly. Crikey. Jeepers. Goodness gracious. Oh dear. Land of Goshen. Yikes. Ugh. Mercy me. Pfft. Humph.

Well, I suppose there is no alternative now but to invite my readers to stand by for a little false teaching. "I think what has happened is this . . . the capital-E Evolutionism that has produced a metaphysical inflation from a proven hypothesis about the physical world to a naturalistic worldview—this modernist teaching *has exposed a flank that perhaps needed exposing*" (31). In other words, one of the things we can learn from Epicureanism is how bad our fundamentalist tendencies are. And one of the reasons fundamentalism is bad, if you harken back to the previous chapter, is that it has unwittingly learned stuff from Epicureanism. If you are not following this, I don't think it's you.

I will mention, but not pursue, the blithe assumption that Wright makes about evolution being "a proven hypothesis about the physical world." This is a striking example of Wright trying to engage with a host of learned adversaries whom he has not read and will not name. He can run circles around an illiterate hedge preacher of seventy-five years ago, and it is the work of a moment to pretend that young earth creationists today are equally rude and equally unlettered. Too bad it isn't the case.

One of the problems with deracinated theology of the kind that Wright is offering us here is the inverse relationship between the loss of theological robustitude and the rise of exciting adjectives. I call these adjectives the flying buttresses of liberalism. "Urgent," "fresh searching," "humble yet powerful," and "fresh insight" come to mind, having read them just recently.

Wright wants the language of Genesis to represent something high and glorious. "This is where we turn toward Genesis 1, toward a fresh reading of image and temple" (32). The calling of Adam is akin to the calling of Israel, and because Wright really is steeped in the language of Scripture, he can fly pretty high when he is talking about the literary part of it. But what does he think all this glorious temple language is actually talking *about*?

> And it leads me to my proposal . . . perhaps what Genesis is telling us is that *God chose one pair from the rest of early hominids for a special, strange, demanding, vocation.* This pair (call them Adam and Eve if you like) were to be the representatives of the whole human race, the ones in whom God's purpose to make the whole world a place of delight and joy and order, eventually colonizing the whole creation, was to be taken forward. God the creator put in their hands the fragile task of being his image bearers. If they fail, they will bring the whole purpose for the wider creation, including all the nonchosen hominids, down with them. (37-38)

True, Eve may have been somewhat hairier than the Sunday school coloring books used to represent her, but that's what we get for relying too much on our memories of Sunday school coloring books.

The glory of the Lord, the shining presence of God, the Edenic Shekinah, descends upon a couple of hominids, whose previous conversation had consisted largely of *ook!* and *ook?* and whose previous activity had included throwing poo out of the trees. What we clearly need around here are some more adjectives. Let's say that the ancient world was *wonderful*. "Basic to his [Paul's] exposition of Genesis is this point: that God put his wonderful world into human hands; that the human hands messed up the project; and that the human hands of Jesus the Messiah have now picked it up, sorted it out, and got it back on track" (35). True, the human hands in the first two instances may not have had opposable thumbs yet, but you can't have everything.

"The root problem we face as Christians is that in articulating a Christian vision of the cosmos the way we want to do, we find ourselves hamstrung because it is assumed that to be Christian is to be anti-intellectual, antiscience, obscurantist, and so forth" (26). Great. Assumed to be that way *by whom*? By the Epicureans running the academy? What Wright wants is a Christian view of the cosmos that topples Epicureanism, and he want to do this to the appreciative applause of the high priests of the Epicureans. Life is hard.

There are two macro problems here—one textual and one theological—and it comes in the form of death. It is the same problem, appearing in two different ways.

First, the apostle Paul identifies death as an enemy to be conquered (1 Cor. 15:54–55; cf. Isa. 25:8), and not as God's central tool for creating mankind. In Paul's theology, Adam brought in death (Rom. 5:12). In Wright's thinking a very long chain of millions of deaths brought in Adam. In biblical theology, Adam is the father of death. In Wright's theology on this point, death is the father of

Adam. "This, perhaps, is a way of reading the warning of Genesis 2: in the day you eat of it you too will die. Not that death, the decay and dissolution of plants, animals, and hominids wasn't a reality already . . . ." (38). So the textual problem is that Paul tells us how death got into the world. He does not tell us how death managed to get Adam into the world.

The second problem, related to this, is how it impugns the goodness of God. God repeatedly calls the world He created *good* (Gen. 1:4, 10, 12, 18, you get the point). Death is bad. This appeasement of Epicurean evolutionists at the front door, allows them to drag the problem of evil in through the back door. But God warned Adam about opening the door to death (Gen. 2:17). To deny that death was the consequence of our sin is to maintain that God likes death, and that He used it to torment millions of animals, turning them into stone for paleontologists to dig up later.

But in my theology, animals get turned to stone by the White Witch, not by Aslan.

THE BUTTERFLY'S BOOTS

I am continuing to work through Wright's book *Surprised by Scripture,* and I now come to Chapter 3, "Can a Scientist Believe in the Resurrection?"

Look. This chapter was *fantastico.* Top drawer. First class. Stupendous. Marvelous. Top flight. Really cool. Fantabulous. This is how Wright deservedly got his high reputation. Am I overdoing it? Too many eggs in the pudding? Just one more. This chapter was the butterfly's boots.

Look. I'll be honest. It really was a great chapter, but I overdid it just a slight little skosh because I looked and saw that the next chapter is going to be on women's ordination. I want to keep an equilibrium going. I have a reputation for evenmindedness to protect.

Look. The previous two paragraphs started with *look*. Writers do that sometimes.

There are three standout features of this chapter that I want to highlight. First, Wright does a great job distinguishing the different kinds of knowing that we must grapple with in discussions like this. Claims about the resurrection are claims about history and so cannot be subjected to strict scientific analysis. "To put it crudely . . . science studies the repeatable, while history studies the unrepeatable" (44). Not only can I not know scientifically that George Washington crossed the Delaware at the Battle of Trenton, it is also kind of important that I not try to know it that way. Having to know about historical events by historical means is not a limitation, at least not for sensible people.

The second point is that Wright plainly shows what the first-century Jews believed about resurrection, and he demonstrates how the early Christians received this set of beliefs and in what respects they modified it. They did not modify what resurrection fundamentally meant, but they did modify other aspects of the traditional Jewish belief. For example, the Jews had room for their Sadducees, but there were no Christian Sadducees. "There is no trace of a Sadducean view, or of that of Philo" (47). Not being a Sadducee was a *sine qua non* of being a Christian in the first centuries—we didn't get our Sadducees until many centuries later. Another example is that while Second Temple Judaism held to the resurrection as part of their faith, the Christians took this faith and made it absolutely central to their faith (v. 47). Wright goes on in this vein and shows five other ways in which the Christians took the Jewish understanding of resurrection and strengthened it in multiple ways. The Christian faith stands or falls with this. If the dead are not raised, we of all men are most to be pitied (1 Cor. 15:19).

Third, Wright has a very engaging discussion of the eyewitness accounts of the resurrection, apparent discrepancies and all, and shows how these features require us to believe that these resurrection accounts are in fact primitive accounts. We have good historical reasons for refusing to believe that these accounts were "cooked." He first points out that the Gospels are saturated with Old Testament citations, but that in the resurrection accounts that drops out—like eyewitnesses who had not taken the time to collate the Old Testament basis for what they had just witnessed. The exegetical basis came later. The second thing is the use of women as the principal witnesses. "Whether we like it or not, women were not regarded as credible witnesses in the ancient world. Nobody would have made them up" (53). They told the story this way because this is the way it had happened, and not because they were laboring to make the story look good. The third point is that Christ's resurrection body was transformed, but not like it was on the Mount of Transfiguration, and not like a shining star out of Daniel. And last, Wright points out that the obvious tie-in to our future resurrection hope is conspicuously not tied in during the course of the resurrection accounts.

Taking all these things together, it seems apparent that the Gospel accounts of the resurrection just dumped the data they had onto the table, in order to give us compelling testimony that cries out to be sorted out. But in the meantime, these accounts are very apparently not polished theologies. They are eyewitness accounts.

There are two concluding observations I would like to make about this chapter. One has to do with what every conservative believer affirms, along with Wright, and the second is something that every conservative believer needs to start affirming, following after Wright.

First, Wright is great on bodily resurrection. He has no use for that species of wishful thinking that wants to evaporate the meaning of resurrection into a warm mist somewhere down in our hearts. Resurrection, for Wright, by definition happens in a very public, physical, tangible, and practical way. Resurrection is something that happens to bodies in history. "Resurrection in the first century meant people who were physically dead becoming physically thoroughly alive again, not simply surviving or entering a purely spiritual world, whatever that might be" (44).

The second thing is something I want to dwell on for a moment. In the comments of one of my previous posts on this book, given the nature of my criticisms, someone asked why we should even bother to read Wright. This chapter is why. This chapter involves more than clearing Wright's orthodox *bona fides* on the question of the resurrection.

I am glad that he is orthodox here, but I am saying something more than that he is okay. I am saying that he is *more* orthodox than many current conservative champions of the "faith once received." I am saying that he is okay in ways that the broad, evangelical wing of the church is not okay. He is healthy in ways that the contemporary Reformed church is unhealthy. On this point, on this particular, there are many conservative believers who need to come to grips with the fact that Wright is *way more orthodox than they are*, meaning that he is more *biblical* than they are, and that he gets the ramifications of the gospel better than they do. Note, I do not say that he gets justification by faith better than John Piper does, because he doesn't, but I am saying that he gets what the *impact* of justification by faith is supposed to be, and he gets it better than the faculties of every Reformed seminary in North America put together.

The resurrection is the transformation of history, and not just a weird event contained within ordinary history, after which ordinary history continues on the way it always did, wandering aimlessly down an amillennial road. And this is something he gets from the Bible, and lots of conservatives don't. And this, incidentally, is why these conservatives keep getting their hineys kicked in our culture wars. American Christians are to be commended for actually fighting the culture war, contra Wright, but they are to be admonished for not fighting with the kind of exuberant and necessary optimism that

Scripture provides for us in the fact of a man coming back from the dead right *in the middle of history*.

> The challenge is in fact that of new creation. To put it at its most basic, the resurrection of Jesus offers itself, to the student of history or science no less than the Christian or the theologian, not as a very odd event within the world as it is, but as the utterly characteristic, prototypical, and foundational event within the world as it has begun to be. (58–59)

> The world cannot cope with a Jesus who comes out of the tomb. who inaugurates God's new creation right in the middle of the old one. (60)

Not only is this true, it is true now. It is happening now. It is transforming all things now, human culture included. Jesus has established in this world a new way of being a human being, and we are all growing up into that. The process has been going on for two thousand years now.

Now, as I grant freely, some of Wright's particular prescriptions for this new way of being human are calculated to give me the screaming fantods. Health care, for example. Wright chides American Christians for their "gut-level reaction against any kind of health-care proposal" (16). *Any* kind of health care proposal, eh? This is not quite my position. I think we should only object to the dumb or tyrannical health care proposals. Other health care proposals are fine.

It is not possible to object to bureaucrat-ridden agencies without reminding Wright of social Darwinism? For some mysterious reason, Wright thinks of things like national health care with affection and respect, and I see nothing but soft despotism. I look at the Veterans Administration scandals, and I see a prolepsis of the kind of treatment everybody is going to be getting shortly, which we and our children deserve because we voted for it. But I decline to believe that we need to have this kind of crappy health care because Jesus rose from the dead and the world is now made new. That seems to me not to follow.

You know what would be cool? We should get a bunch of conservative Calvinists to read *Jesus and the Victory of God*[2], and to do so without being subsequently suckered by all the cool kids of the soft left. We could learn from Wright about the glorious and inexorable nature of the approaching kingdom, straight out of the pages of the *Bible*, and we could do it without forgetting what we learned from Hayek about economics, we could do it without confounding weather and climate, we could do it without capitulating to the siren song of feminist egalitarianism, and we could do it while jealously protecting our continued right to keep and bear arms. Wouldn't that be swell?

2 N.T. Wright, *Jesus and the Victory of God: Christian Origins and the Question of God*, vol. 2 (Minneapolis: Fortress Press, 1996).

We are walking down the kingdom road, but whenever we come to a crossroads, I will always decline to take the left fork. "A wise man's heart is at his right hand; but a fool's heart at his left" (Eccles. 10:2). In other words, the theology of the thing is glorious, but—thank the Lord—the unexamined assumptions of a soft Brit socialism are not entailed in the theology. Jesus rose from the dead, and this *does* mean the gradual transformation of all human history. But it means the gradual transformation of all things for the better. This means that policy proposals that will make everything worse should be ruled out.

But chapters like this one help make things better.

THE ELTON JOHN
VERSION

Wright's chapter on the case for ordaining women starts off a little oddly. He acknowledges that he used to teach that "the creation of man and woman in their two genders is a vital part of what it meant that humans are created in God's image. I now regard that as a mistake" (64).

His reason for considering it a mistake is that Genesis notes that both plants and animals are also divided into male and female (64–65). Now this last observation is quite true, but it is a curious reason for dropping a connection that the book of Genesis explicitly makes. "So God created man in his own image, in the image of God he created him; male and female he created them" (Gen. 1:27, ESV). It would be better, I think, to take this passage as a straight up declaration, and to take the similarities exhibited by the surrounding world as animated typology. The created order exhibits the traits of male and female as a declaration of the glory of man and woman, the woman is the glory of man, who in turn is the glory and image of God (1 Cor. 11:7). Clearly, the mere possession of the male/female distinction is not a sufficient condition for bearing the image of God. But no one ever said that it was.

By the way, for any who want to pursue this a bit further, I have written a small book on the topic, *Why Ministers Must Be Men*[3].

Early on, Wright objects to the way the discussion frequently goes. "Instead of taking texts in a vacuum and then arranging them in a hierarchy, for instance by quoting this verse and then saying that it trumps every other verse in a kind of fight to be the senior bull in the herd (what a very masculine way of approaching exegesis, by the way!), we need to do justice to what Paul is actually saying at this point" (65).

There is some temptation to have a little fun at this point, but I resist it manfully *as* a temptation. But let me share with you what I was tempted to say. I was *tempted* to say, but refrained from saying, that another masculine way of doing exegesis might be to rank verses

3 Douglas Wilson, *Why Ministers Must Be Men* (Monroe, LA: Athanasius Press), 2010.

in a different kind of hierarchy, privileging those texts that are talking about the issue in question, while backgrounding those passages that are about something else. The reason I did not say this is that I know plenty of women who know how to discuss the point at issue and plenty of men who don't. So there's that.

As an example of this quaint procedure, developed by dead male theologians, but applauded by sensible females, suppose we were debating whether or not Og, king of Bashan, had an iron bedstead. One might argue, as I would, that the Pentateuch says that he did (Deut. 3:11). In response, someone else might argue that arbitrary role responsibilities, assigned according to sex, such as the man taking out the garbage, and the woman doing the ironing, is no longer tenable in the light of the full revelation of the gospel in Christ (Gal. 3:28). An example of my hegemonic approach to exegesis would be to privilege Deuteronomy 3:11 over Galatians 3:28 even though I heartily approve of Galatians 3:28.

Speaking of Galatians 3:28, Wright spends some time there, not surprisingly, but argues for something that nobody was disputing, i.e., that women are full members of the body of Christ.

He then offers one line of argument from the fact that "Paul calls a woman named Junia an apostle in Romans 16:7." And so he does. But an apostle is a word that, like deacon, is descriptive of both a function and an office. An apostle is a "sent one," and the sent one has the authority of the one sending, according to the designated purpose. Jesus was an apostle of God, for example (Heb. 3:1). The Twelve were apostles of Christ (Matt. 10:2). Paul and Barnabas were sent by the church at Antioch (Acts 13:3). I myself have been sent out to mow the lawn before.

After spending some time discussing how Mary sat at Jesus's feet, saying that this kind of language is used—as it was with Paul and Gamaliel—for those studying to be rabbis, he goes on to say this: "Like much in the Gospels, this story is left cryptic as far as we at least are concerned, but I doubt if any first-century reader would have missed the point" (70). But this presents a difficulty. The second generation of first century readers, if Wright is correct, did miss the point, massively. Wright has to argue for a form of restorationism here. After the death of the last apostle, this new way of doing ministry in Jesus fell off the face of the earth until it was restored by theological liberals, many centuries later.

His argument from 1 Corinthians 14:34 was contextual. He says that this silence for women was not an absolute ban, because women were instructed to pray and prophecy (1 Cor. 11:2–11). I do agree with him here and think it is a point well taken. He says that in the ancient church, men and women sat separately, and because the message would be in a formal kind of discourse that the women did not know, speaking only "a local dialect or patois" (72), special instructions had to be given. "Anyway, the result would be that during the sermon in particular, the women, not understanding what was going on, would begin to get bored and talk among them-selves" (72), and would have to be told to pipe down.

But this argument, to work, has to assume that the assembly was being led by the males. If this was "a new era in Jesus" running on all cylinders—as Wright argues it was—then how could the new leadership, including women as it now did, be losing the women? Why were the women, on the women's side of the church, unable to follow the reasoning of Philip's daughters? Or of Mary, who was a rabbi who had sat at the feet of Jesus?

Secondly, Wright wants to argue that men and women in leadership in the church should display badges of their respective sexual identities, without confusion. And, as far as that goes, good on him. But that is not Paul's argument. He does not say that the women who pray or prophesy should "look like girls." He says that they should look like they are in submission to their husbands (1 Cor. 11:5). Wright has to argue for more than our egalitarian age is demanding, and for far less than the text requires. That is how you fall between two stools, which is what Wright is doing here.

The *locus classicus* is, of course, 1 Timothy 2:12. The first citation here is Wright's rendering, and the second is from the ESV. Wright's treatment of this is . . . singular.

> They must study undisturbed, in full submission
> to God. I'm not saying that women should teach
> men, or try to dictate to them; rather that they
> should be left undisturbed. Adam was created

first, you see, then Eve; and Adam was not deceived, but the woman was deceived, and fell
into trespass. (1 Tim. 2:11–14)

Let a woman learn quietly with all submissive-
ness. I do not permit a woman to teach or to
exercise authority over a man; rather, she is to
remain quiet. For Adam was formed first, then
Eve; and Adam was not deceived, but the woman
was deceived and became a transgressor. (1 Tim.
2:11–14, ESV)

But in order to get this interesting result, Wright has to
insert words that Paul inexplicably left out. Take, for example, *to God*, and how Wright applies the word *not* to the
invisi-verb *saying*. This is an interesting procedure. "Thou
shalt not commit adultery." Wilson: "I am not saying that
you *should* commit adultery." Sometimes you lose things
in translation, and other times you pick extra things up.

Wright did do two things in this chapter that I appreciated. First, he is clearly trying to prepare his arsenal
beforehand for the next set of battles (on homosexual ordination), and he wants to argue that Paul requires men
and women to maintain "gender differentiation during
worship" (74). "We should certainly stress equality in
the role of women but should be very careful about im-
plying identity" (77). This is like trying to stop a punch
by holding a piece of tissue paper in front of your face,
but I do think it is well-intentioned.

"The underlying point seems to be that in worship it is important for both men and women to be their truly created selves, to honor God by being what they are and not blurring the lines by pretending to be something else" (75). But of course, we live in a time when the blurring of distinctions, particularly sexual distinctions, is being done with a wet sponge, particularly among the Anglicans. And while I think that Wright wants to hold the line there, he has introduced novel ways of translating passages that others may now, with glad shouts of joy, apply to their own projects. Paul said this: "Do you not know that the unrighteous will not inherit the kingdom of God? Do not be deceived. Neither fornicators, nor idolaters, nor adulterers, nor homosexuals, nor sodomites . . ." (1 Cor. 6:9, NKJV). The EJV renders it this way: "I am neither confirming nor denying that the homosexuals and sodomites will not inherit the kingdom" (1 Cor. 6:9, Elton John Version).

But the second thing I appreciated is that Wright recognized, in a number of places, that his case was kind of thin;

> We gain nothing by ignoring the fact that Jesus chose twelve male apostles. (69)

> That's a lot of *perhaps*es. (74)

> I fully acknowledge that the very different reading I'm going to suggest may sound initially as

though I'm simply trying to make things easier,
to tailor this bit of Paul to fit our culture. (79)

Yeah, that sure is what it seems like, but I really appreciate him saying so.

IN WHICH N.T. WRIGHT
DISCOVERS THE MOON
AGAIN

The next chapter from Wright is on eschatology and care for the creation, and it is a mixed bag. The title of the chapter is "Jesus is Coming—Plant a Tree." We will come back to that shortly.

I want to begin by acknowledging what is very good about this chapter, which is Wright's exegetical understanding of the relationship of Heaven and earth, the old creation and the new creation, and what Jesus's resurrection and second coming actually mean for this world. It is very good work, and it is good work from the beginning of the chapter to the end of it. This is basically a chapter-length treatment of his book on the same general topic, *Surprised By Hope*, and has the strengths and weaknesses of that book, mostly strengths.

While there would be quibbles here and there, I don't want to dispute with his exegesis on this topic. I think it is good. I think it salutary. I think it is most necessary for our generation of evangelicals, particularly in America, to recover this understanding. Anything that Wright does to help this along is something I am all for. I am grateful for his influence here at this point.

But this leads to the second issue. While his exegetical theology is fine, his historical theology is atrocious. I have no problem with how Wright argues his biblical case in this chapter because, as it happens, I am a postmillennialist. The position that Wright is advancing has a name, and it is a name that Wright appears to be extremely reluctant to use. I have not read everything Wright has written, for the age of miracles is past, but I have read a lot of his stuff. I am open to correction here, but I don't recall him ever using the term *postmillennialism*, still less identifying with it. This could be fine—albeit a little weird—except for the next thing.

Last week Sam Allberry tweeted this: "' . . .and only I am left'—The prophet Elijah and every book by N T Wright."[4] In a previous post, I said that Wright has an annoying habit of announcing discoveries that all of Western theology has missed when in fact his discoveries are

4   Sam Allberry (@SamAllberry), Twitter, first week of June 2014, https://twitter.com/SamAllberry. Content no longer available.

nothing of the kind. He is like a very competent amateur astronomer who keeps discovering the moon. We could put up with this, but then he keeps chiding *us* for having missed it. Now it is true that there are popular schools of theology that have missed it, but Wright is here making claims about the broad history of theology, and he gets it spectacularly wrong.

Here is an example from this chapter, but there are other little comments like it scattered here and there. And it is why somebody once coined the word *insufferable*. "It is my belief that the broad sweep of Western theology since way before the Reformation, and continuing since the sixteenth century in both Roman Catholicism and the various branches of Protestantism, has been subbiblical in its approach to that potent combination of themes, eschatology, and ecology" (83).

But in actual fact, the broad sweep of Protestant eschatology, from shortly after the Reformation down to the beginning of the nineteenth century, was postmill. The point here—for my non-postmill readers, love you all—is not whether or not postmillennialism is correct, but whether it was held by anybody significant who was contained within Wright's dismissive "broad sweep of Western theology." Anybody heard of Jonathan Edwards? B.B. Warfield? David Livingstone? William Carey? Iain Murray was right to label this as the *Puritan* hope. Anybody out there heard of the Puritans? Geez Louise, Tom.

Wright does have a lot to say that is valuable. He has something to contribute, and he does have unique insights to contribute. But his habit of planting his flag on the beach of thickly inhabited lands is really bad for his ethos. He looks like Columbus planting the flag in the modern Bahamas, right next to the shaved ice stand. True, Chesterton discovered orthodoxy as though he were the first one there, but he had the good grace immediately afterward to recognize that the joke was on him.

Here he is again. Speaking of Romans 8:18–27, Wright makes this astonishing claim: "And yet, as I say, preachers, commentators, and theologians in the Western tradition, both Catholic and Protestant, have almost routinely regarded this section as something of a distraction" (87).

This hope is glorious, and I exult in it. But when I was becoming postmill, I learned a great deal about how to understand Romans 8 from a number of saints in the Western tradition. I give thanks for them all, and I want to declare my indebtedness to them. I don't want to pretend, with Wright, that they never existed.

The third point to make concerns one possible reason why Wright puts distance between himself and standard-issue postmillennialism. The last word in the quote cited above was *ecology*. When it comes to policy prescriptions, the actual things that one would do to make the planet that Jesus is coming back to a better place, Wright tends toward soft leftism. That was not the case with the broad swath of postmillennialists in history. In other words, the impact of postmill Christians up to this point has not really been leftist in any recognizable way.

But I would argue it has been a practical blessing precisely because of that.

In this chapter, Wright's practical politics are not foregrounded, but they are hovering in the background, and to my mind, ominously (83, 85–86, 95, 106).

I said that we would return to the issue of planting trees. In my day I have planted many trees, and I have some thoughts on the subject. I am all for it. Jesus is coming, and we should plant a tree. But this is not a new idea. Martin Luther is quoted as saying, "If I knew the world would end tomorrow, I would plant a tree today."

But . . . how? What kind of tree? Who paid for it? Who owns the dirt where we will plant it?

I want the tree that is planted to have been purchased by the planter himself at Home Depot, and purchased there with his own money. I want no taxpayer to have been soaked for the expense. I want to praise personal responsibility and praise the suburbs while I am at it. Learn how to plant your own hedge, and learn how to take care of it. Every man under his own fig tree, every man mowing his own lawn.

I do want the earth to be transformed into a garden city, and I want it to be emerald green. This means keeping the statists far away from it. I have no problem with being green. My difficulty is that our modern priests of Baal always promise us green and, just like in the days of old, turn everything brown.

We can't do that—turn everything brown—and we can't because Jesus is coming again. The saints with Him in glory now say that the intermediate state is not their home. They're just passing through. And when they get back here with Jesus, at the true marriage of Heaven and earth, we should not want this planet to look like a badly-run VA hospital. Because Jesus is coming, this means we need to learn how to love liberty. And we need to have the Spirit teach us to hate statist coercion.

Jesus is coming. Hug a logger. And plant a tree.

FORGETTING THE
COLUMNS

The next chapter is on the problem of evil, and in it Wright says something that is particularly fine. Since there are a lot of other problems, to be dealt with in due course, I wanted to begin with the praise.

"The Gospels tell this story in order to say that the tortured young Jewish prophet hanging on the cross was the point where evil, including the violence of terror and the nonhuman forces that work through creation, had become truly and fully and totally itself. The Gospels tell the story of the *downward spiral* of evil" (121).

In this statement, and a number of related statements in this chapter, Wright does what he does best, which is to set and describe the broad context—the events leading up to the cross are set center stage in a cosmic drama, which is right where the cross belongs. He does this very well, and no complaints on that score.

The approach that Wright takes to the problem of evil generally appears to be a variation of the *Christus Victor* approach to the cross, which is absolutely biblical and fine, but only so long as other key elements of biblical atonement theology (e.g., propitiation) are not left out, which Wright unfortunately does.

What Wright says about the silencing of the principalities and powers is glorious and right and true. Christus Victor is one biblical aspect of the death of Christ. But it is not the whole thing. To write about God's vindication of His righteousness without using the word *propitiation* is like building a replica of the Parthenon and forgetting to put in the columns. For someone like Wright to miss this concept in Paul, and in the New Testament, is simply fatal to his project.

On this topic, Wright continues to indulge his propensity for calling things new that are not new at all. For example, he thinks we are dealing with "a new problem of evil" (110). But what's new about it? People have been dying in tsunamis for many centuries. People in anguish, also for centuries, have wanted to know why. This question has been asked forever by poets and wailing widows, and not just by metaphysicians. But Wright dismisses the older concerns as the stuff of philosophical fustian, with more than a whiff of the constant seminar room, the one with a particularly metaphysical fly buzzing helplessly against the windowpane of inscrutability—"older ways of talking about evil tended to pose the puzzle as a metaphysical or theological conundrum" (111).

Wright, by way of contrast, wants to locate the problem as one we struggle in the midst of as opposed to it being a problem we can somehow "solve." "If we think we've solved the problem of evil, that just shows we haven't understood it" (114).

"Theologies of the cross, of atonement, have not in my view grappled sufficiently with the larger problem of evil as normally conceived" (119). Wright sees tight theological reasoning as insufficient grappling. Specific detailed answers seem to him to be pat answers, by definition. By contrast, he steps back and tries to give us the grand panorama, setting it in marked opposition to "philosophical" treatments.

> What the Gospels offer is not a philosophical explanation of evil—what it is or why it's there—but the story of an event in which the living God deals with it. (122)

> He has taken the weight of the world's evil on his own shoulders. This is not an explanation. It is not a philosophical conclusion. (123)

He is right that it is not a philosophical or metaphysical explanation. It couldn't be, because it is not any kind of an explanation at all. The problem with the grand panoramic vista is that if you get high enough up on the ridge you can't hear the screams in the valley—and the glorious story you are telling becomes mere hand waving.

When that happens, your attempted account simply turns into a jumble of contradictions. For example, in some ways, Wright acknowledges God's mastery of the macro-scene. "God declares throughout scripture that he is going to put the world to rights at the last, even though this will involve, in Haggai's phrase, giving both heaven and earth one last great shake to sort everything out" (115). A moment later he adds that "humans need to be put right and the world needs a good shake" (115).

Up on the ridge, this simply sounds like a biblical citation. Who could be against that? The problem is that when God picks up heaven and earth and shakes it, a bunch of bones get broken. It is kind of rough for those of us who have to live inside this thing. But then, just a few pages later, Wright wants to say that God's work in the world is from within it—with evil as a larger backdrop to the whole thing. "Rather God loves his world so much that, faced with evil within it, he works within the world, despite the horrible ambiguities that result" (117).

So God steps into the world, in order to confront evil face to face. And this is quite biblical—that is precisely what He does. His name is Immanuel. God reveals Himself to us in Christ on the cross. But He does not do this in a way that relinquishes His sovereign and majestic control over every particle of His created order. When we see Christ on the cross in faith, we see that the wisdom of the Father is infinite. We should *not* see that the wisdom of the Father is stuck down here with us, caught with us in the machinery.

But in Wright's theodicy, this sovereignty is precisely what God does relinquish. Wright rejects "a God who sits upstairs and pulls the puppet strings to make things happen, or not, as the case may be, down here" (126).

When disaster strikes, God is a first responder—"the God who rushed to the scene with all the help he could muster" (126–127). The difficulty here—and it is a grave difficulty—is that in our undeniable experience, God does not show up with "*all* the help" He could muster. He just doesn't. This is what causes the problem of evil. God either can't help or won't help. If He can't help, He isn't God. If He won't help, then He must have a good reason. We must wait patiently for the unfolding of that reason, and telling ourselves lies in the meantime won't help us deal with it.

I would want to justify God in the unfolding of the story. This is not just in the grand story, but also in all the lesser stories as well. I need to know that God has a point to all this when it comes to the things that I and those dear to me have to go through. Is Romans 8:28 true in our case, or not? And if true, in what ways? But Wright doesn't like this line of thinking at all. "Nor can we say that evil is good after all because it provides a context for moral effort and even heroism, as though we could get God off the hook by making the world a theater where God sets up little plays to give his characters a chance to show how virtuous they really are. That is trivializing to the point of blasphemy" (115).

Patient endurance is not blasphemy. The riches of God's goodness and forbearance and patience are meant to lead us to repentance (Rom. 2:4). It is by patient continuance in doing good—even in the midst of trial and affliction—that we are to seek glory, honor, and immortality. In other words, personal salvation is a big deal in Paul—an essential part of grand panorama. There is nothing blasphemous about it. "And thou shalt remember all the way which the Lord thy God led thee these forty years in the wilderness, to humble thee, and *to prove thee, to know what was in thine heart*, whether thou wouldest keep his commandments, or no" (Deut. 8:2).

On subjects like this, Wright says that he waves off "easy answers," but his whole theology of the thing is nothing more than minced theology, with euphemism abounding. For example, he refers to the Israelites and their "deeply ambiguous entry into the land" (117). From the tone and flow of this chapter, it appears that he is speaking of the slaughter of the Canaanites. The Israelites were the people of God, and yet their way with the sword was attended by lots of problems and ambiguities. However, the text, the Scriptures, would agree that there were ambiguities in Israel's obedience, and would point in another direction entirely. Their problem was that they didn't kill enough Canaanites. Saul was the one who let Agag live, losing his kingdom thereby, and it was Samuel who came along and created all that ambiguity—well, ambiguity for twenty-first-century academics. There was no ambiguity that Agag could detect.

Speaking of ambiguities, Wright says that when God steps into the world to fight evil, that too creates ambiguities. But what are these ambiguities? Are they anything like horrors and outrages? And who is responsible for the horrors and outrages? This world is all screwed up. Whose idea was it? The world is one messed-up place, and everyone who believes in *ex nihilo* creation believes that it was God's idea to put it here. I am just speaking for myself here, and I might get shouted down, but there are really only two options when it comes to this particular dilemma—atheism or Calvinism.

But in response to this problem, Wright defends his platitudes by pointing out the possibility of platitudes elsewhere. "How, after all, does a hymn like 'There Is a Green Hill Far Away' have anything at all to say to a world dumbstruck in horror at the First World War, Auschwitz, Hiroshima, 9/11?" (120).

Here are some of the lyrics of the hymn he is referring to.

> There is a green hill far away,
> Outside a city wall,
> Where the dear Lord was crucified,
> Who died to save us all.

Now I grant that this is not poetry off the top shelf, and that the expression of truth here is hackneyed, the way it goes with hymns sometimes. But the woman who wrote it did so when she was dealing with a seriously sick daughter. And it does have something to say to a dumbstruck world, because the only unbiblical claim in those quoted words is the color of the hill. "Jesus Christ died to save sinners" *can* be said in clichéd ways, and so the claim can be easily dismissed by those who have had to deal with various horrors. Job's comforters can say a lot of true things. When that happens, we should repent by stopping our manufacture of true sayings out of presswood—*in order to say the same thing in silver*, refined seven times.

And last, and very importantly, it is here on this topic that we find Wright pulling back from the ramifications of his earlier settlement with theistic evolution. He wants a young earth theodicy without actually having to have a young earth. Read this carefully: "But I find it somewhat easier to suppose that the project of creation, the good world that God made at the beginning, was supposed to go forward under the wise stewardship of the human race as God's vicegerents and image bearers, and that when the human race turned to worship creation instead of God, the project could not proceed in the intended manner but instead bore thorns and thistles, volcanoes and tsunamis, the terrifying wrath of the creation that we humans are treated as if it were divine" (126).

Now I think that this statement is exactly correct. But in an earlier chapter, Wright denied the basis of this view. Not only that, but he also said that those who insisted on this view, the one he now espouses, were guilty of false teaching.

I argued in an earlier installment that Adam brought death into the world, and I denied that death brought in Adam. Adam gave us death. Death did not give us Adam. This, in contradiction to Wright's earlier suggestion that God selected a couple of hominids (whom we could dub Adam and Eve, but only if we liked), in order to promote them up to human.

But notice what he says in the quotation above. He says that God created the world "good," and that after the human race turned to worship the creation, this brought in the nasty stuff. *Now* we had to deal with thorns and thistles, volcanoes and tsunamis, and other manifestations of the "terrifying wrath of the creation." But earlier, in chapter two, the clear implication was that all this "wrath" had been munching the hapless hominids for tens of thousands of years. Is Wright saying there were no volcanoes before the Adam-hominid? No—"not that death, the decay and dissolution of plants, animals and hominids wasn't a reality already" (38).

Poetry can get you out of many a jam, but I don't think it can deal with this one. Either "nature red in tooth and claw" is a good thing, or it isn't. If it is good, then why is Wright calling it wrath now? And wrath for what? If it is not good, then why did God call it good, and use it in the creation of man?

But biblical poetry might be able to do it. Wright can get poetry to do a lot of heavy lifting. Poetry even divided the Red Sea. Speaking of that great deliverance, Wright says this: "As later poets look back on this decisive moment in the story of God's people, they celebrate it in terms of the old creation myths: the waters saw YHWH and were afraid, and they went backward" (108).

This does not diminish the element of the miraculous. Not at all. The horse and rider were thrown into the Ugaritic milieu.

CAESAR AS COXCOMB

Given how hard I have been on Wright for most of these chapters, it might seem remarkable to some that I have now come to what I consider to be the second outstanding chapter of this book. Others might think the word *remarkable* is not the right word. Perhaps the word *schizophrenic* is the one we are looking for. This would leave unresolved whether we are talking about Wright's intellectual schizophrenia or mine. I will leave you to discuss that among yourselves. Be judicious.

I should mention one nice little thing he did before moving on to discussing why this chapter was so good. Early in the chapter Wright was fair-minded enough to quote something I said to him at lunch the one time we met. There was a gang of us there in Monroe when he spoke at the Auburn Avenue Pastors Conference in 2005. And if he was only going to quote me once, I am happy with the line he chose. "As a friend of mine from out West says, 'In Idaho "gun control" means you use both hands'" (130). How that figures into the theme of this chapter you will have to work out on your own time.

In this chapter, Wright outlines three important ways the Bible addresses modern Western culture. The first is that biblical thinking requires us to get rid of our natural tendency to "split-level" dualism. Second, Wright is insistent—contra the postmodernists—that we must learn to see the Bible as "an overarching story, a single great narrative, which offers itself as the true story of the world" (143). And third, he shows how the Bible teaches us to *know*. At the end of the day, epistemology is a function of love. His discussion on all three points was quite satisfying, really good, and worth the price of the book.

But better than that, early in the chapter he clearly articulates the only possible foundation for this kind of thinking.

> Let me put it starkly. *The Bible tells the story of the world is having reached his destiny, its climax, when Jesus of Nazareth came out of the tomb on Easter morning.* The Enlightenment philosophy, however, *tells the story of the world as having reached destiny, its climax, with the rise of scientific and democratic modernism.* These two stories cannot both be true. World history cannot have two climaxes, two destinies. (137, emphasis his)

> The point is that *the resurrection, if it had oc-*
> *curred, would undermine not only the Enlighten-*
> *ment's vision of a split world but also the Enlighten-*
> *ment's self-congratulatory dream of world history*
> *reaching his destiny in our own day and in our own*
> *systems.* (138, emphasis his)

This is so good. It is glorious. It is the foundation that enables us to say that Jesus is Lord and that Caesar isn't. It also a truth that places my disagreements with Wright in an appropriate context. Indeed, because this is true—*wonderfully true*—it gives me purchase when I want to argue the particular applications with Wright.

And this brings me back to my joke about gun control. Why am I so opposed to gun control? Because Jesus is Lord, and Caesar isn't.

Wright remarks that American Christians are good at "bundling the issues" (130). But when you turn the page, he says, *rightly*, that modernity "splits the world into two" (132). But which is it? Should we bundle or should we split?

Now as he notes, there is a way of bundling that saves the bundler from the burden of having to think. But there is also a bundling that is the result of integrated world-view thinking, where everything is woven together—in a tight weave—in a desire to bring every thought into submission to Christ. When Owen Barfield said of C.S. Lewis that what he thought about everything was contained in what he said about anything, this statement is taken as high praise, as it should be. We don't dismiss Lewis as a "bundler."

This is why I praise Wright's political theology highly, and why I dissent from his practical politics violently. *Jesus is Lord, and Caesar isn't.* Once we have said that, we still have to determine what it means in the details. Jesus is Lord, and Caesar isn't, and we are now standing at a crossroads. Which direction would Jesus have us go? The answer to that question must not be assumed without debate. The answer to that question is too important to simply let the zeitgeist breezes, that always tend to blow to the left, determine it for us.

What does Jesus say about it? What does that Bible teach? We must know that since Jesus is to be our ruler, it is necessary to never forget that He is not a silent ruler. He wrote a book, and we must always resort to that book. We must resort to that book in the details. If we do not, then we are simply using a Jesus cardboard cutout for Caesar to stand behind. And He did not rise from the dead in order to be a cardboard cutout.

So this is precisely why, in my view, we shouldn't allow Caesar to lay claim to vain, Canutian attempts to control the weather, why we shouldn't allow Caesar to take our guns, why we shouldn't put Caesar in charge of our health care, why we shouldn't let Caesar define what marriage is, why we should reject Caesar's incessant bloodlust, why we shouldn't let Caesar hector the children about what a healthy lunch is, why we must insist that Caesar stay completely away from wages and prices, and so on. Because Caesar is a conceited coxcomb, and because Dickens taught us that the law is an ass, the "and so on" list is quite a bit longer than this one here.

Which means we have a lot of work to do. When pouring the concrete for the foundation of that work, Wright is enormously helpful. His concrete truck is great. I just object to using the concrete truck when we are installing the kitchen cabinets.

WHAT THE PIMP
NEEDS TO DO

In this installment, I want to commend Wright yet again, briefly summarize what he says, and then try to supply a key element that I think he is missing. Were he to gain that element, either from me or from a *reputable* dealer, I believe the good points he is urging here would gain a great deal of additional potency. So I am not really disagreeing here, but since the next chapter is on politics, I think I might resort back to this chapter in order to explain our anticipated differences there.

The chapter is titled "Idolatry 2.0," and it is quite good. In it, he points out rightly that every kind of nature abhors a vacuum, not just physical nature. Whenever you banish the gods, others come creeping back in. "But history shows again and again that other gods quietly sneak in to take their place" (152).

Three of the most obvious gods in our day are Mars, Mammon, and Aphrodite—war, money, and sex. In a nice touch, Wright associates these three gods with their respective prophets—Nietzsche, Marx, and Freud. Each of those guys would sit on their tall three-legged Delphic stools, get the fumes into their heads, and start raving about how it was all about "power," or "economics," or "sex." He then has a good discussion of the various forms of worship these gods receive in our day, and I commend the chapter to you. There is good stuff here.

The thing missing from Wright's discussion of this is that he doesn't make the obvious connection between all three of these gods and the modern high priest of that pantheon, which is the modern state. All three of these religions are tax-supported religions, and there will be no reformation unless and until we cut off Caesar's money supply. These religions have an *apparatus*, and that apparatus is the modern state. Repentance would mean that the state would have to shrink back to a more normal size—about twenty times smaller than it is now.

So this means that thoughtful reform requires us to analyze the state's role in propitiating each of these gods. War is obvious, and the big state/big business collusion that I call crapitalism is also obvious, and the government's promotion of sexual perversion should be obvious. There are a lot of people talking about how pedophiles often groom their prospects beforehand, and that really is something every parent should be aware of. But they should also be aware that the government schools are just a gigantic grooming program.

The state is able to do these things only because it suctions up a gargantuan amount of our money, and is swollen beyond every boundary of common decency. Pose the question to yourself another way. Work it out in a thought experiment. What would happen if every North American devotee of Mars, Mammon, and Aphrodite truly and completely *repented*? I will tell you what would happen. The government would shrink drastically.

When the whores repent, the pimp needs to get an honest job.

BET YOU A CAN OF CORN

I should begin by saying that this bit of writing is not a rant. I can assure you that at no time in the composition was the screen spittle-flecked. I remained in a good humor the entire time. And I mention all this because it is my intention to step out a bit, high, wide, and handsome. My criticism of Wright at this juncture is going to have a little tang to it. My adjectives and my metaphors are going to be slathered in West Texas barbecue sauce. That one, for instance.

The title of this chapter is "Our Politics Are Too Small," when the actual problem is that our politics are far too large. If responsible government were considered as two or three of those little marshmallows, the kind you put into Jell-O for the kids, our modernist concept of idolatrous government is that marshmallow puff monster at the end of *Ghostbusters*.

True, our cultural vision *is* truncated and pinched, and much of what Wright is arguing here could be used to broaden that vision—but he doesn't do it. If, under the lordship of Jesus, our *politics* assumed a more reasonable size and shape, our *culture*, free of coercion, and also under the lordship of Christ, would be in a position to truly flourish.

But Wright doesn't do this. He is like the constables in *Penzance*. "We go, we go, we go!" "But you *don't* go!" Let me 'splain.

First, Wright is absolutely correct that the gospel of our Lord Jesus Christ is necessarily political. Jesus rose from the dead in the middle of history, and so the old ways of doing politics must be abandoned. This happens progressively in history, not all at once. Building on the foundation of the resurrection, the Church is God's plan for getting this task done, and He is willing for it to take a while. And those who hold to power in the old ways don't want to let go of it. "God acting in public is deeply threatening to the rulers of the world in a way that gnosticism in all its forms never is" (173). The "political implications [are] inevitable" (163). Wright correctly stands against the notion "that God doesn't belong in public life" (164, 169).

The *structure* of his position is marvelous, but what does he fill it up with? Picture a four-hundred-year-old bookcase, made out of seasoned walnut, the kind you can easily find in the part of the world Wright lives in, crammed full of bodice-buster romances, the kind you can find in the part of the world I live in, like at Safeway.

To his credit, Wright does invites scrutiny of his position. "We could do with a similar analysis of the political setting of all Gospel criticism, my own included" (174). Okay. Let's do this thing then. I am just going to swing from skyscraper to skyscraper here, like basic mistakes were buildings, and book reviewing had somehow given me spider powers.

He begins with an irrelevance. "In Britain, the issues are bundled up in different ways than in America" (164). So? If we must reject the split thinking of Heaven/earth dualisms, let us practice by rejecting any dualisms caused by the Atlantic. Jesus was the one who rose, so we don't care how Americans bundle things. Jesus conquered death, and so the Brit bundling is also a nullity, theologically speaking. How does *Jesus* bundle them? Let's answer *that* question, from the Bible, and then call it the Christian worldview.

Then he does something really odd, and he does it repeatedly, throughout the chapter. "I want to suggest that the Bible enables us to navigate a path of wisdom not just halfway between secularism and fundamentalism but on a trajectory that shows up those ugly brothers as simply missing the point, representing two opposing wings of a now thoroughly discredited worldview" (165, cf. pp. 166, 170, 174, 180).

In another place he calls fundamentalism a "conservative analogue" to gnosticism (172). All this is just pulled out of a hat somehow. He defined secularism very clearly (and very well), but the closest he gets to a definition of fundamentalism is a slight hint at the top of page 173. With his reference there to the rapture and Armageddon, he appears to be saying that Christian fundamentalism is simply dispensationalism. Readers of this blog know that I am no dispensationalist, but let's be fair to them. I mean, crikey. If you are going to say that the most materially oriented saints you ever saw are gnostic analogues, then please, an argument would be nice.

But, having done this, he *then* says, "You won't be surprised that I believe such a way can be found by returning to the foundation documents of the Christian faith, in particular the four Gospels" (167).

Returning to the foundations, eh? Kind of like recovering the fundamentals? Apparently there must be a way to affirm stuff without falling into the "shrill certainties of fundamentalism" (180). I wonder what makes it shrill. These are deep imponderables. How do we declare that Jesus rose without sounding like those *other* people who really think that?

Next building. Whoosh. Wright quotes Jim Wallis to the effect that he grew up in an evangelical church never having heard a sermon on the Sermon on the Mount (167). This kind of story is very sad, and that lack of early training certainly shows. If we don't teach children the meaning of the Sermon on the Mount, they might *never* find out.

Coming to the next point, Wright makes an astute observation about certain tendencies in Gospel criticism that then leads to his central confusion. "The Gospels have thus been seen either as a social project with an unfortunate, accidental, and meaningless conclusion, or as passion narratives with extended introductions" (169). In other words, liberals don't get that death and resurrection stuff, and conservatives can't figure out the monga-preamble to the death and resurrection stuff.

But notice what Wright does next. It is done very deftly, and if you weren't paying attention, you might not notice it. "Those who emphasize his death and resurrection do their best to anathematize any attempt to continue Jesus' work with and for the poor" (170).

This understated slam amounts to a misbegotten slander, and it reveals the heart of all the confusions that are going on in Wright's analysis. There are two sides to this. First, Wright apparently doesn't count it as compassion unless Caesar is standing there with a gun at your temple. Private generosity doesn't count for *anything* because opposition to food stamps, say, amounts to a repudiation of any mercy ministry whatsoever.

So let's talk about that. "Anathematize *any* attempt" to feed the poor? Let's consider for a moment who really cares—to borrow a phrase from Arthur Brooks' fine book of that title[5]. When it comes to private philanthropy, private generosity, the kind of giving that is not spurred on

5 Arthur C. Brooks, *Who Really Cares: The Surprising Truth About Compassionate Conservatism* (New York: Basic Books), 2006.

by Caesar and his shiny coercion gun, who really cares? I will tell you. Americans are far more generous than Europeans. Inside America, the red states are far more giving than the blue states. Christians of every stripe are far more generous than secularists. Protestants are more generous than Catholics. Evangelicals are way more generous than the Protestant mainliners, and I would be willing to bet a can of corn for your next food drive that dispensationalists are at the very top of this particular food bank chain.

They are also least likely to vote for a candidate who will, if elected, send people to your house with guns and big block letters on their windbreakers after the IRS has determined you have been Insufficiently Generous. Keep in mind that dispensationalists are the *least* likely to correctly identify the beast of Revelation (who was Nero), but *most* likely to correctly identify all the contemporary beast knock-off brands.

Wright is correct to note that Christ's program for this world calls for "radical *personal* moral demands" (173, emphasis mine). But let me say this again. I am not tired of saying it. Personal moral demands of this nature do not flow from the barrel of a gun. *That's not how mercy works. That's not how compassion goes.* Hiring Smith (with Murphy's money) to extort more money from Jones so that Winston can give it away to Cooper *is not compassion.* And putting Murphy and Jones in chokey until they start feeling the love is not what Jesus was urging in the Sermon on the Mount. And never forget that Jim Wallis is the one who eventually gets us SWAT teams out of that sermon, and they might even shoot your dog. C.S. Lewis once mentioned the kind of preacher who, if his text had had small pox, wouldn't allow his sermon to catch it.

On paper, Wright is aware of the possibilities of governmental abuse. He mentions the "hermeneutic of suspicion that we rightly apply to anyone in power" (169). He says this, but he doesn't *do* it. Nary a suspicion anywhere.

"Human power structures are the God-given means by which that end is to be accomplished—otherwise those with muscle and money will always win, and the poor and the widows will be trampled on afresh" (175). So what happens when the ones with muscle and money send lobbyists to hobnob with the great and powerful? When was the last golf game that Obama played with a poor widow? When governments put privilege up for sale, it will always be the muscled money that buys it. What did you *think* would happen? And the way you fight this is not through some joke of a legal reform that puts a law on the books that says government privilege will always be sold to the *lowest* bidder. Good luck with that. The way you fight it is by establishing a government—as we used to try to have—that is not permitted to sell privilege to anybody, at any price. And the only way to do that is by reducing the size of government to such a libertarian extent that Jim Wallis starts having nightmares, with personal freedom and responsibility riding down upon us like the galloping horsemen of the Apocalypse.

Now to reduce the size of government, incidentally, you must reduce the caloric intake. Get, in other words, between the hogs and the bucket. You must buy a rattlesnake flag for your truck and attend Tea Party rallies. You must think that David Brat is a pretty okay guy for a liberal.

So Wright does acknowledge that there is "satanic possibility of tyranny" (176). But I think he must be thinking of goose stepping armies and missile parades. What about soft despotism? What about the nanny state? To modify Mencken, what about those who think America is a gigantic milch cow, with three hundred million teats?

Quoting Kofi Annan, Wright says "we urgently need to develop ways of holding governments, especially powerful governments, to account" (179). Huh. This is Boromir-talk. When *you* get the Ring, you will take it back to Gondor, and you will put safeguards in place. There will be a Review Commission. You will establish a Council of Advisors. There will be periodic audits, conducted by responsible civil servants. We should let Sir Humphrey be the chair.

You actually hold powerful governments to account by throwing their damned ring into Mount Doom.

So then. Jesus is Lord. Jesus has risen. Because of this, our task is not to try to get this swollen government of ours to go on the right path. Nor should we want it to go on the left path. We should tell it—in the name of Jesus, mind you—to go on a diet.

Printed in Great Britain
by Amazon